P9-DXL-225

Profiles in American History

The Life and Times of

ELI WHITNEY

Mitchell Lane
PUBLISHERS

P.O. Box 196 · Hockessin, Delaware 19707

Titles in the Series

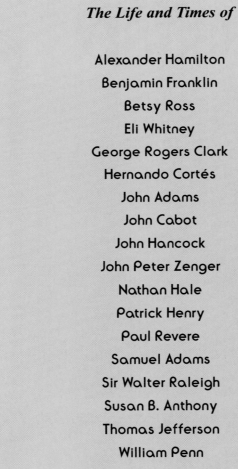

Profiles in American History

The Life and Times of

ELI
WHITNEY

Karen Bush Gibson

Printing   1   2   3   4   5   6   7   8   9

Library of Congress Cataloging-in-Publication Data
Gibson, Karen Bush.
    The life and times of Eli Whitney / by Karen Bush Gibson.
        p. cm. — (Profiles in American history)
    Includes bibliographical references and index.
    ISBN 1-58415-434-9 (library bound : alk. paper)
    1. Whitney, Eli, 1765–1825—Juvenile literature. 2. Inventors—United States—Biography—Juvenile literature. I. Title. II. Series.
TS1570.W4G47   2006
609.2—dc22

                                                                    2005028498

ISBN-10: 1-58415-434-9   ISBN-13: 978-1-58415-434-1

ABOUT THE AUTHOR: Karen Bush Gibson was drawn to Eli Whitney's problem-solving abilities. She believes that his ability to take a complex problem and turn it into a series of manageable steps led to Whitney's being one of the greatest inventors of all time. Writing extensively in the juvenile educational market, Karen's work includes biographies, current events, and cultural histories, such as *The Life and Times of Catherine the Great*, *The Fury of Hurricane Andrew*, and *The Life and Times of John Peter Zenger* for Mitchell Lane Publishers.

PHOTO CREDITS: Cover, pp. 1, 3, 22, 36—Superstock; pp. 6, 18, 20, 32, 34, 40—Library of Congress; p. 12—Yale University Gallery; p. 16—*New England-Primer*; pp. 38, 41—Jamie Kondrchek; pp. 25, 28—Fritz Goro/Time-Life Pictures/Getty Images; p. 39—Hulton Archive/Getty Images.

PUBLISHER'S NOTE: This story is based on the author's extensive research, which she believes to be accurate. Documentation of such research is contained on pages 43 and 46.

The internet sites referenced herein were active as of the publication date. Due to the fleeting nature of some web sites, we cannot guarantee they will all be active when you are reading this book.

To reflect current usage, we have chosen to use the secular era designations of BCE ("before the common era") and CE ("of the common era") instead of the traditional designations BC ("before Christ") and AD (*anno Domini*, "in the year of the Lord").

Profiles in American History

Contents

*For Your Information

Eli Whitney designed a simple machine that mimicked hands removing seeds from cotton. Wires held on to the seed while the cotton was pulled through rollers. The machine, called the cotton gin, was capable of cleaning ten times more cotton in a day than one person could.

CHAPTER 1

Ten Days That Changed the World

The twenty-six-year-old man clutched the rail as he boarded the ship in the New York harbor. He was beginning to doubt whether now was the best time for his first sea voyage.

"Allow me to offer you some assistance," a man next to the rail said. He steadied the shaky younger man and led him to a chair next to a well-dressed woman. She jumped up and covered him with a blanket.

"Are you quite all right, sir?" she said.

He smiled his thanks. "Yes, I'm afraid I haven't recovered as much as I would have liked from my smallpox inoculation. They say you shouldn't travel without it, but I hadn't known it would make me this weak. . . ."

"Perhaps you should travel at a later date?"

"I'm to start a new job as a tutor on a Southern plantation. I am expected," he said.

The other man grinned. "What a coincidence. My name is Phineas Miller. I started as a tutor for the Greene family. Allow me to introduce Mrs. Greene."

"It's nice to make your acquaintance. I am Eli Whitney."[1]

Eli Whitney had planned on being a lawyer after graduating from Yale College in September 1792. But first things came first. College had been expensive, and he had debts to repay. Whitney

had taught children before attending college, so working as a tutor was nothing new for him. He hoped it would also give him the opportunity to study law in his free time.

The ship set sail for Savannah, Georgia. While Whitney grew stronger each day, he enjoyed the company of Catharine Greene and her five children. A widow, Mrs. Greene had been visiting relatives in the North for the summer, probably in Rhode Island, where she and her late husband had originally come from. Now she and her family were returning home. Home was a plantation called Mulberry Grove that sat alongside the Savannah River in eastern Georgia. The plantation had been given to her husband, General Nathanael Greene, in gratitude for his military service during the Revolutionary War against England. Mulberry Grove started as a farm for mulberry trees used in the silk industry. It later became one of Georgia's leading rice plantations. The Greenes moved to Mulberry Grove in 1785. General Greene died of sunstroke less than a year later.

Like Whitney, Phineas Miller was also a Yale alumnus. Formerly the family's tutor, he began managing the estate after the death of General Greene. Three years after Whitney's first visit to Mulberry Grove, Phineas and Catharine Greene married.

Whitney arrived with his new friends in the southern port city of Savannah. Although autumn, the weather was still warm and humid. Soon after disembarking from the boat, he learned that he was jobless. The tutoring position had been given to someone else. Mrs. Greene liked the polite young man and wanted to help him.

An 1832 memoir by fellow Yale student Denison Olmsted reported: "Mrs. Greene kindly said to him, my young friend, you propose studying the law; make my house your home, your room your castle, and there pursue what studies you please."[2]

Whitney studied law books during his first winter in Georgia, so different from the winters he was used to in Massachusetts and Connecticut. He looked for ways to return the kindness Mrs. Greene had shown him. He had always had a talent for fixing things and had been doing so all his life. The Greene children (George, Martha, Cornelia, Nathanael Ray, and Louisa) were thrilled that he could fix their broken toys, and even more delighted with the new toys he built for them.

When Mrs. Greene complained that her circular embroidery frame known as a tambour tore the threads, her grateful houseguest made her a new type of frame. Whitney's frame held the fabric without tearing the embroidery stitches. It worked wonderfully.

Mulberry Grove often had visitors, including George and Martha Washington, who had befriended the Greenes during the American Revolution. One day, neighboring plantation owners visited Mulberry Grove. Many were men who had served under General Greene. The talk soon turned to their troubles in growing a profitable crop. The chief crop of the South, tobacco, was problematic. It was so harsh to the soil that crop rotation was necessary to give the soil a chance to replenish itself. An added problem was an oversupply of tobacco.

The plantation owners needed a new, profitable crop. Rice, indigo, and corn were grown in the South, but the demand for these products wasn't large enough to sustain a region of large plantations. Planters had hoped cotton might be the answer to their financial troubles, as the demand for cotton was high. But few farmers had found a way to profit from the short, scrubby plant. Farmers who grew long-staple or black seed cotton along the coast did well. Also known as Sea Island cotton, this type of cotton grew only in sandy soil. The inland variety grown throughout most of the South was green seed cotton. It took too much time to clean the fibers of the sticky green seeds. In fact, it took one person all day to remove the seeds from just one pound of cotton. The planters grumbled that green seed cotton was about as helpful as weeds in a Southern plantation. What was needed was a more efficient means of removing the seeds.

Catharine Greene understood their concerns. "Gentlemen," said Mrs. Greene, "apply to my young friend, Mr. Whitney. He can make anything. I have accomplished my aim. Mr. Whitney is a very deserving young man, and to bring him into notice was my object."[3]

Whitney reported that he had never seen cotton or cotton seed. Since he enjoyed a challenge, he went in search of green seed cotton with the seeds intact. It was late winter, not growing season, so he scoured the warehouses in Savannah until he found a batch of raw cotton.

Cotton is a short, scrubby plant. When ready for harvest, the plant puts out balls of cotton. The seeds must be removed from the cotton before the fibers can be spun and the yarn woven into cloth.

He returned to Mulberry Grove and told Phineas Miller of his plans. Miller encouraged him, giving him a room in the basement to use as a workshop. Whitney gathered what tools were available and made the rest of what he needed. Only Phineas and Mrs. Greene knew what Eli was doing during the long hours he spent in his workshop. The Greene children were consumed with curiosity.

Whitney studied the manner of removing the seeds by hand. One hand held the seed while the other hand pulled at the lint. He decided he could duplicate this process with a machine. He made a sieve of wires to hold the seeds. For pulling the cotton from the seed, he made a long cylinder, or drum, with small hooks that would rotate close to the sieve. These hooks caught the cotton. A faster rotating brush then cleaned the cotton from the hooks. In only ten days, Whitney had made a model of a machine that combed the sticky green seeds out of cotton.

A temporary building was built near the house for the machine. Mrs. Greene invited men from all over Georgia to see the model. With an expectant audience in place, Whitney put some cotton into the hopper. Soon after he started to turn the rollers with the hand crank, clean cotton appeared. The planters saw a simple yet ingenious machine capable of cleaning ten times more cotton than the old way of doing it by hand. The cotton engine, referred to as the cotton gin, was born. It became one of the most revolutionary inventions America has ever seen.

"Cotton Is King"

"Cotton is king," declared Senator James Hammond of South Carolina as he addressed the Senate in 1858. Cotton certainly ruled the South during the nineteenth century. The economy of the Southern states depended on cotton and the use of people as slaves in order to make the crop profitable. Disagreements about slavery and states' rights had already led to increasing tension between the North and South. Hammond's words angered many senators from the North.

The cotton plant is thousands of years old. The earliest evidence of cotton use comes from India and Pakistan around 3000 BCE. The Indians of Mexico and Peru were using cotton by 1000 BCE.

By the 1500s CE, England was importing raw cotton from Mediterranean countries. Workers turned cotton into cloth through spinning and weaving. American colonists began growing cotton in the early 1600s for their own use. Large-scale cotton production began after Eli Whitney introduced the cotton gin.

Suddenly, the South became a wealthy place, full of opportunities. And it wasn't the only place that benefited from the cotton gin. After it was picked and seeded, cotton was shipped to textile mills in the northern United States and England. Domestic exports in 1825 came to just under $67 million. Over half of what was exported was cotton. In 1791, the United States produced two million pounds of cotton. Fifty-two years later, U.S. cotton production was one billion pounds.

The growing season for cotton is the longest of any crops planted each year, taking five to seven months from planting the seed to picking the cotton. Fields are cleared and prepared in the first few months of the year. Cotton seed is planted around the end of March. In July, cotton starts blooming. When the plant matures, golf-ball-sized fruit on the

Spinning and weaving cotton

plant splits open to reveal cream-colored down with lots of seeds. The cotton is then picked and shipped to a cotton gin.

Cotton is mainly used to make cloth for clothing. It has become one of the most common fabrics used to make clothing in the world.

*Ezra Stiles was president of Yale from 1778
to 1795. As the college's seventh president, he
influenced many men, including Eli Whitney.
He was respected as an important American
theologian, yet his interests were varied and
included science, law, and philosophy.*

CHAPTER 2

Mechanical Genius

Eli Whitney was born December 8, 1765, to Eli and Elizabeth Whitney. His grandfather, John Whitney, came to America from England in the first half of the 1600s. John Whitney's family settled in Massachusetts, where they earned a reputation as good farmers. Elizabeth Whitney's family also emigrated from England. According to biographer Denison Olmsted, the mother's great grandfather had been a successful man in England. He called his five sons together and told them: "America is to be a great country; I am too old to emigrate to it myself, but if any one of you will go, I will give him a double share of my property."[1]

The youngest son, Elizabeth's grandfather, agreed to go and arrived in Boston, Massachusetts. He became a landowner, as did his sons. Elizabeth's father, John Fay, moved to Westborough and started a family. Located in Worcester County in central Massachusetts, near the Assabet River, Westborough (also known as Westboro) became the 100th town in Massachusetts in 1717. It continued to draw more settlers and prospered during the 1700s.

Eli grew up on his parent's farm in Westborough as the oldest of four children. He had one sister and two brothers. Eli's father was a successful farmer, and there was always work to be done. He was also thrifty; he did not waste time or money. When Eli was only five, his mother became ill, and he took on more of the household

chores. During winter, he tended to the sixty cattle before walking a mile to the one-room schoolhouse.

Reading was difficult for Eli, and he developed a reputation as a slow learner. He didn't learn how to read until he was twelve years old.[2] But that didn't stop him from learning. He worked as hard in school as he did at home. He found that he enjoyed working with numbers, which came easier to him than words. Eli spent time observing people at work and asking them questions. He had a good memory for how things worked. While still a child, he had accumulated quite a bit of knowledge.

Many Westborough farms included workshops for making things the household and farm needed. Eli's sister, Elizabeth, reported that Eli could often be found near the workshop. He worked with any type of material, including wood and iron. Elizabeth remembered, "Our father had a workshop, and sometimes made wheels, of different kinds, and chairs. He had a variety of tools, and a lathe for turning chair-posts. This gave my brother an opportunity of learning the use of tools when very young."[3]

At eight years old, Eli was consumed with curiosity about his father's watch. He just had to know how it worked. One day when no one was around, he took the watch apart and examined the many tiny pieces. Even more amazing was that he was able to put it back together. He had answered the burning question of how a pocket watch worked. His father didn't learn what he had done until Eli told him several years later.

In 1777, Elizabeth Whitney died giving birth to a son. She was thirty-six years old. Afterward, Eli spent even more time in the workshop. It was a place where he felt at home, and he preferred tinkering to farming. One day, he decided to make a violin, or a fiddle, as it was often called. Musical instruments were usually made by experienced craftsmen, but Eli did such a good job that he soon started repairing violins for the people of Westborough. His skill in making many things was said to exceed that of experienced artisans. He regularly astounded neighbors with his knowledge and abilities. It was as if he had a special gift for anything mechanical. Though tall with big shoulders and hands, Eli had a gentle manner that people liked. He often took care of his brothers and sister.

Mr. Whitney married Judith Hazeldon when Eli was thirteen. In addition to a stepmother, the boy now had stepsisters too. His stepmother didn't know of Eli's genius in fixing things until one of her prized table knives broke. Eli made her a new one. The only difference was the lack of a stamp on the handle. He told his stepmother that if he'd had the right equipment, he could have also duplicated the stamp.

The American Revolution raged on in nearby Boston, approximately forty miles from Westborough, during Eli's childhood. Boston is known as the birthplace of the Revolutionary War, with many battles and skirmishes taking place there. Although too young to fight, Eli found other ways to contribute.

Eli found a need and filled it. According to Olmsted, "This being the time of the Revolutionary war, nails were in great demand, and bore a high price."[4] Nails were made by hand in those days, unlike today's machine-made nails, which are produced at a rate of more than 500 per minute. But the first machine to make nails wouldn't appear until 1851. Still in his teens, in 1781 Eli obtained a forge and began making nails. He had to hammer them by hand from a bar of hot iron. He made nails when he wasn't busy with the farm, usually in the winter months. Once he began a project, he paid attention to little else until his job was finished. He made quite a bit of money for his father with his new business.

According to historian Harold Evans, "By fifteen, he was an embryonic capitalist. Having seen what the market would pass, and what he could produce on his own, he calculated that his profit margins justified taking on labor."[5] Eli took off on horseback one day and visited neighboring towns until he found an assistant to help with the making of nails. His business had expanded.

When the war ended, England again began supplying nails to the newly independent country of America. There was no longer much demand for Eli's nails. He noticed a new fashion with ladies' hats. Instead of tying bonnets under the chin, women were using hatpins to attach the hats to their hair. Whitney began making hatpins—he may have been the only hatpin maker in the colonies at the time. He later added well-crafted walking canes to his business.

The New-England Primer *was a textbook used in colonial America to teach the alphabet. Eli Whitney used it with his students.*

By the time Whitney turned nineteen, he knew that the life of a farmer wasn't for him. He decided he wanted to attend college. His stepmother opposed the idea, and others agreed with her. Some said that such mechanical genius as Whitney's should not be wasted on college. His father thought Whitney too old, plus the costs for college were high.

Whitney persisted in his plans. He continued earning money making repairs to whatever people brought to him. He also made seven dollars a month by teaching school in Westborough and in the nearby towns of Grafton, Northboro, and Paxton. He taught in

one-room schoolhouses, where he'd build a fire every morning so that the children would stay warm. He taught from texts like *The New-England Primer* and *Noah Webster's Speller*. During the summer, he prepared for college by attending Leicester Academy in Grafton. Whitney, at age twenty-three, entered Yale College older than most of the other students.

Whitney worked hard at his college studies during his three years at Yale. He was elected to the academic honor society, Phi Beta Kappa. He preferred writing about political ideas over literary works. His writings often showed logic and reasoning, and he occasionally brought a vivid imagination to the subject. He particularly enjoyed mathematical and mechanical studies.

Olmsted reported that Whitney begged to use the tools of a carpenter working at the building where Whitney lived while at Yale. The carpenter was hesitant to allow a student access to his tools, but eventually he did. Olmstead wrote of the encounter: "But Mr. Whitney had no sooner commenced his operations, than the carpenter was surprised at his dexterity, and exclaimed, 'there was one good mechanic spoiled when you went to college.'"[6]

In his free time, Whitney liked to walk the streets of New Haven, Connecticut. A harbor city originally settled by the British in 1638, it exported various farm products and imported sugar and molasses from the Caribbean islands. The Eli Whitney Museum reports that at the time, "there was a growing number of workshops that attracted Whitney, including a soap factory, Abel Buell's mint, an optics shop and Amos Doolittle's copper-engraving shop."[7]

One day, a professor mentioned an experiment that he unfortunately couldn't show to his students because the equipment was broken and had to be sent off for repair. Whitney asked for a chance to repair it and did so to the satisfaction of the professor. He soon began making other repairs for the faculty; often he made his own tools also. Whitney's mechanical aptitude became well-known around the campus. Yale's president, Ezra Stiles, was delighted when Whitney fixed a planetarium device that was used to teach movement and positions of the planets. Stiles would become a lifelong friend and advocate of Whitney.

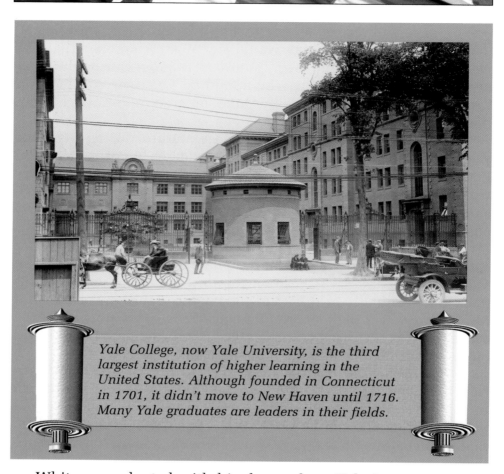

Yale College, now Yale University, is the third largest institution of higher learning in the United States. Although founded in Connecticut in 1701, it didn't move to New Haven until 1716. Many Yale graduates are leaders in their fields.

Whitney graduated with his degree from Yale in 1792, accomplishing what many had doubted he could do. Although he had often been encouraged to find a career that would make use of his mechanical talents, he wanted to be a lawyer. His education had demonstrated that he enjoyed using reasoning to problems. To be a lawyer meant more studying. Working as a tutor seemed to be the perfect solution . . . until he created the cotton gin.

"Old Eli"

Yale was founded in 1701 when ten Connecticut clergymen decided to make a gift of books to found a college. Later that year, the General Assembly of Connecticut approved a charter for the Collegiate School. From 1702 to 1707, classes met in the home of Rector Abraham Pierson at Killingworth.

The school moved to New Haven in 1716. After two years, its only building was still unfinished due to a lack of funding. A retired merchant named Elihu Yale donated money to the school in 1718. In appreciation, the school was renamed Yale College and, later, Yale University. Yale's nickname is "Old Eli" after Elihu. The school grew both in size and reputation.

Connecticut Hall

The Yale campus now covers about 310 acres. The redbrick Connecticut Hall built in 1752 is the only building that remains from colonial days. College freshmen live in the area of the old campus. As the third oldest university in the United States (Harvard and the College of William and Mary are older), Yale has much to boast about. It is home to the oldest university natural history and art museums. The college newspaper, the *Yale Daily News*, was founded in 1878 and is the oldest college newspaper in the United States.

The Yale Library owns around eleven million books, including an impressive collection of rare books and manuscripts, making it one of the largest college libraries in the world. It is also the home of the papers of Eli Whitney, donated by his great-granddaughters: Susan Brewster Whitney, Elizabeth Fay Whitney, Henrietta Edwards Whitney Sanford, Anne Farnam Whitney Debevoise, and Frances Pierrepont Whitney Knight. Yale Library received these gifts in 1941 and 1953. The Eli Whitney papers consist of letters and business papers relating to the cotton gin, the Whitney Armory, and personal papers.

Many leaders in business, the arts, and politics are Yale graduates. Five U.S. presidents graduated from Yale, including William Taft and George W. Bush. A large number of university presidents are Yale graduates. Noted actresses Jodie Foster and Clare Danes are also Yale graduates.

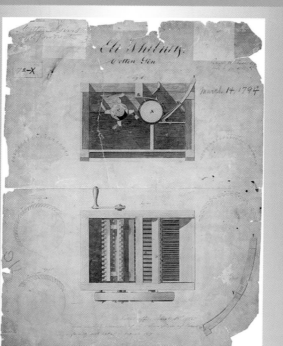

Eli Whitney was awarded patent 72-X for the invention of the cotton gin The patent was supposed to protect his rights as creator of the cotton gin for fourteen years. Instead, Whitney spent most of that time engaged in legal battles. He never patented another invention.

CHAPTER
3

The Cotton Gin Patent

The country of India has a long history with cotton. A churka was the first device used to gin cotton. This type of cotton gin separated seeds from the lint by pulling cotton through a set of rollers. It worked well enough in the United States with the long-staple cotton grown on the coast, but most of the South grew short-staple cotton. Another gin called the rolling gin was sometimes used in the South. This device didn't remove the seeds, it only crushed them. The cotton from the roller gin was inferior to that which came from Whitney's cotton gin.

After Whitney's demonstration of the cotton gin, planters rushed to their fields to plant green seed cotton. Word-of-mouth about the new invention that would change the cotton industry spread throughout the South. Whitney still wanted to study law, but Miller encouraged him to go into business.

Miller and Whitney formed a partnership to market the cotton gin. Their contract, dated May 27, 1793, stated that if the cotton gin were successful, "the profits and advantages arising therefrom, as well as all privileges and emoluments to be derived from patenting, making, vending, and working the same, should be mutually and equally shared between them."[1]

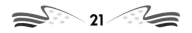

Eli Whitney enjoyed solving problems. When Mrs. Greene asked for his help in creating a better way to clean or remove seeds from cotton, he isolated himself. He examined cotton and the hand-cleaning method. After ten days, he had created a model of the cotton gin.

Instead of selling cotton gins, their plan was to develop ginning stations throughout the cotton-growing area. The partners would charge planters 40 percent of the cotton in order to gin it. Miller was certain they would be rich. He began looking for locations to place their cotton gins. Whitney left for the North to build cotton gins and to obtain a patent.

A patent is a document from the federal government granting an inventor exclusive rights to an invention for a limited time. In Whitney's era, the period was fourteen years. Now, it is twenty. A

patent gives an inventor, or any other owner of the patent, the right to prevent others from making, selling, importing, or using the invention in the country that granted the patent.

The first patent laws under the Constitution allowed two government officials the power to issue a patent to anyone who presented a written description and a model, and paid a fee. The officials who originally authorized a patent were the Secretary of State, Secretary of War, or the Attorney General. Today, patents are administered by the United States Patent and Trademark Office. The first patent was awarded in 1790 to Samuel Hopkins of Philadelphia for improving the making of potash, an ingredient in soap, glass, and fertilizer. According to the patent office, by 2006, a patent was being granted every three minutes.

After building and perfecting his next cotton gin, Whitney presented his application for a patent to Secretary of State Thomas Jefferson in Philadelphia (where the government was located at that time) on June 20, 1793. An outbreak of yellow fever in Philadelphia delayed the patent approval.

While he waited for the patent to be approved, Whitney returned to New Haven, Connecticut, where he had attended college. New Haven had become his adopted home and where he would live for the remainder of his life. He got busy building cotton gins for the South.

Miller encouraged Whitney to work fast. He wrote to his partner: "It will be necessary to have a considerable number of gins made, to be in readiness to send out as soon as the patent is obtained, in order to satisfy the absolute demand, and make people's heads easy on the subject, for I am informed of two other claimants for the honor of the invention of cotton gins, in addition to those we knew before."[2]

Unlike the hand-cranked model he had built at Mulberry Grove, Whitney's larger gins were built to be powered by horses or water. Under this type of power, these cotton gins could do the work of fifty people. Thomas Jefferson was so fascinated by Whitney's cotton gin that he asked for more sketches and information about the invention. Then Jefferson ordered one for himself. Meanwhile, Whitney received patent number 72-X on March 14, 1794. With

the patent in hand, Whitney and Miller believed success was right around the corner. Unfortunately, success eluded them.

The summer of 1794 saw outbreaks of yellow and scarlet fever in New Haven. Approximately 114 people died, and finding workers to build cotton gins became difficult. Another setback developed when a fire destroyed the cotton gin factory on March 11, 1795. Twenty machines plus various incomplete cotton gins were destroyed. Over the next seven months, Whitney retooled his factory and began building more cotton gins. He accomplished much in a short amount of time, but there had been too many delays: awaiting the patent approval, yellow and scarlet fever outbreaks, and the fire.

By 1796, Whitney and Miller placed thirty gins in eight locations throughout Georgia. Most of them remained still and empty. Counterfeit cotton gins had turned up in Georgia after someone stole Whitney's model from Mulberry Grove (copies of the model now sit in the Smithsonian Institution). Like many of Whitney's ideas, the design for the cotton gin was simple and easy to copy. Planters had become impatient; many had fields ready to be picked long before Whitney's cotton gins arrived. There were also strong objections to the high fee Miller and Whitney had set to gin the cotton. Some of the imitation gins had small changes from Whitney's and were claimed as new inventions.

Phineas Miller filed lawsuits against individuals for patent infringement. The first case went to court in 1797. He and Whitney were disappointed when the jury voted against them. The partners would spend all of their resources going to court. During the many hearings, they listened to various arguments meant to destroy their reputations. Unknown people spread false rumors that Whitney's cotton gin damaged the cotton fiber. One argument was that Whitney was not the first inventor of the cotton gin. Rumor had it that someone in Switzerland had come up with the idea first. Witnesses would claim they had seen cotton gins years earlier in England and Ireland. Rarely were specific names used in these accounts, and none of the rumors could be proven. Interestingly, England, with its many textile mills, did not appear to prosper

The cotton gin revolutionized the economy of the United States. The South grew the profitable plant and seeded it. Cotton was then shipped to the North and turned into cloth. It became the chief exported product, earning the country millions of dollars.

from the cotton produced from cotton gins until after the introduction of Whitney's invention.

More than sixty suits were filed in Georgia before Whitney and Miller received a favorable decision. By this time, several years had passed, and bankruptcy loomed over them. Both men had borrowed money, sometimes at very high interest rates of 12 to 25 percent, to build cotton gins. Money was also needed to buy land for the ginning stations and to pay for all the court costs.

Struggling to get out of debt, the partners agreed to sell the patent rights. An inventor may sell all or part of an invention's patent for a fee, or charge royalties based on sales, or both. Whitney and Miller contracted with South Carolina, North Carolina, and Tennessee. South Carolina was the first, promising to pay the partners $50,000 for use of the cotton gin. North Carolina followed in 1802 by putting a tax on using the cotton gin. Taxes collected would go to Miller and Whitney. Tennessee passed a similar tax the next year. Unfortunately, news came that South Carolina was canceling their contract. Georgia never contracted with Whitney and Miller. In the meantime, Miller died on December 7, 1803, of

blood poisoning. He would never see the success he had worked so hard for.

Patent fights continued until 1807, when Whitney's patent was finally validated. At this time, the courts established Whitney as the true inventor of the cotton gin. In all, he won only about $90,000, barely enough to cover his many debts.

An occasional legal adviser for Whitney wrote to Olmsted that he had "never seen such a case of perseverance, under persecution: nor do I believe that I ever knew any other man who would have met them with equal coolness and firmness, or who would finally have obtained even the partial success which he had. He always called on me in New York, on his way to the South, when going to attend his endless trials and to meet the mischievous contrivances of men who seem inexhaustible in their resources of evil. Even now, after thirty years, my head aches to recollect his narratives of new trials, fresh disappointments, and accumulated wrongs."[3]

The South prospered for many years because of the cotton gin. Cotton output quadrupled in the first four years after the gin was introduced. In 1792, the United States exported 138,328 pounds of cotton; in 1794, the year Whitney patented his gin, 1,601,000 pounds were exported; the following year, 6,276,000 pounds; and by 1800, the production of cotton in the United States had risen to 35,000,000 pounds, half of which was exported. By the mid-1800s, America was the world's largest supplier of cotton.

When he applied for patent renewal in 1812, Whitney told Congress that because of the cotton gin, cotton gave the South more profits than any other crop and "that as a labour saving machine it is an invention which enables one man to perform in a given time that which would require a thousand men without its aid, to perform in the same time."[4]

The patent renewal was denied. Although no other invention changed an industry as greatly and as quickly as the cotton gin had, Whitney made no money on the invention. He later said, "An invention can be so valuable as to be worthless to the inventor."[5] Eli Whitney never tried to patent another invention.

Thomas Jefferson

Thomas Jefferson is best known for writing the Declaration of Independence—but that was just the beginning of his fifty years in public service. Jefferson served as governor of Virginia from 1779 to 1781, and in 1785 succeeded Benjamin Franklin as minister to France. Newly elected president and friend George Washington asked Thomas Jefferson to be the first Secretary of State in 1789. He later served as vice president under John Adams before becoming the third president of the United States in 1801 and serving for two terms. During Jefferson's presidency, the United States almost doubled in size, largely due to the Louisiana Purchase. Jefferson sent two men, Lewis and Clark, to explore the West. The slave trade was also banned during his term.

This tall, red-haired Virginian attended the College of William and Mary and studied law. He was far more comfortable writing about liberty than speaking about it publicly. He was thirty-three when he wrote the Declaration of Independence. He later wrote another bill he was very proud of, the bill advocating religious freedom in Virginia, which was passed in 1786.

Thomas Jefferson promoted self-government along with freedoms supported by the Constitution and the Bill of Rights. His beliefs are often referred to as Jeffersonian democracy. He was a founder of the Democratic Party.

Jefferson's Monticello home

Although Jefferson is most remembered for this many years in politics, he was also an architect and farmer. His home was in Virginia, where he was born. His favorite place in the world was his beloved Monticello, which he'd had built on a mountain. In addition to designing Monticello, he also designed the University of Virginia and the Virginia State Capitol.

Jefferson enjoyed and encouraged art and music. He played his violin in chamber music concerts occasionally. His more than 6,700 books later formed the beginning of the Library of Congress.

Like Eli Whitney, Jefferson enjoyed inventing. Among his inventions were an improved type of plow, a decoding device, and a lap desk. He created the concept of dollars and cents that we use today.

Jefferson died on July 4, 1826, at his Monticello home.

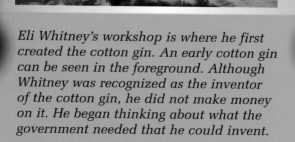

Eli Whitney's workshop is where he first created the cotton gin. An early cotton gin can be seen in the foreground. Although Whitney was recognized as the inventor of the cotton gin, he did not make money on it. He began thinking about what the government needed that he could invent.

CHAPTER 4

The Father of Mass Production

After more than ten years of defending the patent to his cotton gin in courtrooms of the South, Whitney was frustrated. Yet he was also a reasonable man who understood that at least part of the problem was that he and Miller had tried for a monopoly on the cotton gin business. Realizing he would not make money on the cotton gin, Whitney began thinking about other ways to make money. One of his ideas was to make a screw press to print stamps for the United States government. What the government really needed, though, were muskets.

France, an ally during the American Revolution, was unhappy that America had resumed relations with the British. War with France seemed imminent, and the United States government wanted to be prepared. The government had voted to spend $800,000 for weapons. The most popular guns of the day were muskets made of wrought iron; steel was too expensive in the late 1700s. In 1798, muskets were made individually, each one handcrafted by a skilled gunsmith. As each musket had about fifty pieces, it took a lot of time to make just one.

The government had armories at Springfield (Massachusetts) and Harpers Ferry (West Virginia), but neither armory made more than 1,700 guns a year. In order to have enough weapons to fight a war, the government needed to contract with private armories

as well. Whitney knew very little about muskets, but he knew how to fill a need. He had already developed a reputation as the inventor of the cotton gin. When asking for the contract, Whitney wrote to Secretary of the Treasury Oliver Wolcott: "I am persuaded that Machinery moved by water adapted to this Business would greatly diminish the labor and facilitate the Manufacture of the Article. Machines for forging, rolling, floating, boreing, Grinding, Polishing, etc. may all be made use of to advantage."[1]

The government contracted with twenty-seven individuals, including Whitney, to provide muskets like the French Charleville model. Whitney's contract of January 14, 1798, was the largest contract—10,000 muskets in 28 months. He would be paid $13.40 for each musket. Four thousand guns were expected at the end of the first year. "Mechanical invention, a sound judgment, and persevering industry, were all that he possessed, at first, for the accomplishment of a manufacturing enterprise, which was at that time probably greater than any man had ever undertaken, in the State of Connecticut,"[2] wrote Olmsted.

The first order of business was to find a location for his new armory. Water power was necessary to his idea. He found the right place about two miles outside of New Haven near the Mill River. He purchased Christopher Todd's old gristmill. Winter delayed construction, but by May 1798, the main factory building had been finished, along with a dam and waterwheels.

Whitney's next goal was to find workers. He attempted to draw skilled gunsmiths from the cities by providing housing. Gunsmiths learned the craft of forging, carving, and shaping a musket in a long apprenticeship. Because of the skill needed, gunsmiths were few, especially in America. Most guns came from Europe, where countries placed a high value on the rare skills of gunsmiths.

Whitney had no choice but to hire unskilled workers. He found that they were easier to train. "My intention," he claimed, "is to employ steady sober people and learn them the business. I shall make it a point to employ persons who have families, connections, and perhaps some little property to fix them to the place—who consequently cannot be easily removed to any considerable distance."[3] He hired sixty workers with little experience and then

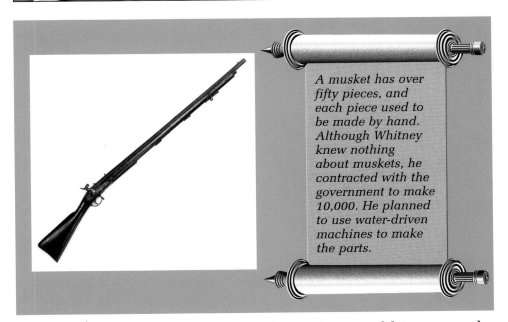

A musket has over fifty pieces, and each piece used to be made by hand. Although Whitney knew nothing about muskets, he contracted with the government to make 10,000. He planned to use water-driven machines to make the parts.

trained them to operate the machinery that would turn out the many different parts of a musket.

Visitors to the Whitney Armory in the early days were more likely to see machines being built than muskets. Whitney made a pattern for each part of the French Charleville musket to use as a model. He then made machines that would cut and shape the parts. One of these was the filing jig, which used a guide for the workman's file and a guide to show where to drill up to a dozen holes. Workers started the machines, did the filing (in the beginning), and put the pieces together. Built using Whitney's method, musket parts would be interchangeable. This not only made the process of making muskets faster, but allowed for easy repair if they broke. For example, the firelock mechanism on a musket sometimes became damaged. Using Whitney's method, fixing it was simply matter of putting a new firelock in an old musket.

Making a musket entailed a lot of steps. According to the Eli Whitney Museum, in 1825, "195 separate operations in musket production were listed in a report about Springfield Armory, and were identified as performed by hand or by waterpower."[4] Basically, the process could be boiled down to shaping and cutting.

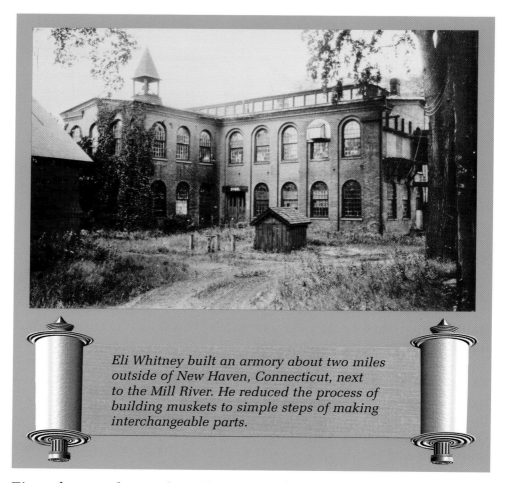

Eli Whitney built an armory about two miles outside of New Haven, Connecticut, next to the Mill River. He reduced the process of building muskets to simple steps of making interchangeable parts.

First, the metal was shaped with high heat. The east bank of Mill River had the forge for the shaping. On the other side of the river were the machines and tools for cutting the metal, the second stage of making a musket. One improvement that Whitney made to the musket was to make the pans out of brass instead of iron so that they wouldn't rust after contact with gunpowder.

Whitney's ten-year-old nephew, Philos Blake, described the factory in a letter to his sister Betsy in September 1801: "There is a drilling machine and a boring machine to bore barrels and a screw machine and two great large buildings, one other shop and stock-

ing shop to stocking guns in [*sic*], a blacksmith shop and a trip hammer shop, and five hundred guns done."[5]

What went on inside the two large buildings of the early armory? Very little is known about the machinery used at the armory before 1825. Whitney did not write descriptions of his machinery. Unlike the cotton gin, no model existed because Whitney had vowed never to apply for another patent. None of the machines has survived into present times, although approximately 35,000 muskets from this time period did. Most are in museums or private collections.

Perfecting the manufacturing process took time. According to Whitney, "A good musket is a complicated engine and difficult to make—difficult of execution because the conformation of most of its parts correspond with no regular geometrical figure."[6]

Instead of delivering 10,000 muskets in twenty-eight months, it would take eight years to complete them. Only 500 muskets were delivered in the first year instead of the expected 4,000. In 1801, Whitney was summoned to Washington, D.C., to explain the delay. He showed up with a box of parts to ten muskets. He demonstrated the system of interchangeable parts to government officials, who were astonished with its ease. The ability for guns to be repaired quickly and easily would be a bonus for the army against an enemy.

In 1812, Whitney was awarded another contract from the federal government for 15,000 guns. These he delivered in two years. He also supplied guns to the state militias of New York and Connecticut. Whitney had no shortage of people willing to speak well of him and his armory. According to Denison Olmsted, Governor Tompkins of New York proclaimed Whitney's establishment to be the most perfect he had ever seen.

American guns received a lot of attention at the London World's Fair held in 1851. Britain began using the same system at its Royal Small Arms Manufactory with machinery from the United States. "It has generally been conceded that Mr. Whitney greatly improved the art of manufacturing arms, and laid his country under permanent obligations, by augmenting her facilities for national defence,"[7] Olmsted wrote. After Whitney perfected the

Eli Whitney was so successful in his system for building guns in America that his methods spread throughout the world. American guns were introduced at the 1851 London World's Fair (above). Soon, Britain began using the same system.

manufacturing process, he applied what he learned at the two public armories and saved the government $25,000 annually.

The Whitney Armory would be a major force in weapons manufacturing for ninety years, and Whitney's methods of manufacturing continue to be used. Some of his designs for machines were used in other manufacturing processes that made objects from iron and steel.

Eli Whitney had devised the first system of mass production, sparking the beginning of the Industrial Revolution.

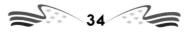

Whitneyville

After Whitney built the armory, he set about creating a village to support the armory. With the same attention to detail, he built at least ten other structures. One of the first was a boardinghouse at the corner of Whitney Avenue and Armory Street. Many of the single workers stayed at the boardinghouse.

Munson's Portrait of Whitneyville

Married workers lived along Armory Street in homes made of native stone. Whitney may have been the first employer in America to build houses for his workers. After building his own home, he built shops. One of the most important buildings in the village was the barn. The village depended upon agriculture for their food, and the barn housed the animals and tools needed for farming.

This village became known as Whitneyville. Located just north of New Haven in a scenic valley, it sat alongside Mill River, which met Long Island Sound a few miles away. Whitneyville soon became a model for other New England villages. In 1827, William Giles Munson painted a portrait of Whitneyville. It shows an organized community in harmony with the hills and Mill River.

As functional as Whitneyville was when it was first created, its purpose had been served. Thirty-five years after Whitney's death, a new dam was built. Roads were rerouted and buildings torn down. The Whitney Armory was sold to Winchester Arms Company, one of New Haven's largest employers, in 1888. The Mill River became New Haven's first public water source. A picturesque Lake Whitney was created. Little of Whitney's town survived. The remaining houses were torn down in 1912. Nearby Hamden was incorporated, and what was left of Whitneyville became part of it.

The Eli Whitney Museum was founded at the site. The barn once used to house cows and pigs is now used for summer theater productions and dances. The New Haven Colony Historical Society and the Yale University archaeology program have on different occasions excavated the armory site to find more clues about the Whitney Armory and Whitneyville. Most of what has been discovered comes from a later period, when Eli Whitney's son ran the factory.

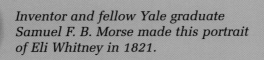

Inventor and fellow Yale graduate Samuel F. B. Morse made this portrait of Eli Whitney in 1821.

CHAPTER
5

A Visionary

Eli Whitney devoted large amounts of time to his work and the factory, but he valued family and friends. A very likable man, Whitney had many friends who enjoyed his company. He corresponded with his brother, Josiah, who was a merchant in Boston. He was close to his sister, Elizabeth Whitney Blake, and took a special interest in his nephews, Philos and Eli Whitney Blake. He saw to their education. At a young age, the nephews loved to spend time at the factory. They would later run the factory for Uncle Eli. They took after Eli and became inventors too. They invented an architectural lock called the mortise lock. Later, their stone-crushing machine was used to pave roads. They weren't the only inventors in the family. A grandnephew, George Eli Whitney, would have more than three hundred patents for inventions, including the first steam-powered automobile and a bicycle brake.

In 1817, at age fifty-one, Whitney finally married. His wife, Henrietta Edwards, was twenty years younger. She was the daughter of a Connecticut district judge, the Honorable Pierpont Edwards, and granddaughter of a legendary preacher, Jonathan Edwards.

After living as a bachelor for so long, Whitney was delighted to start a family. He and Henrietta moved to a house at 275 Orange Street. Eli applied his inventors' mind to his household and continued to find things that needed inventing, including a special

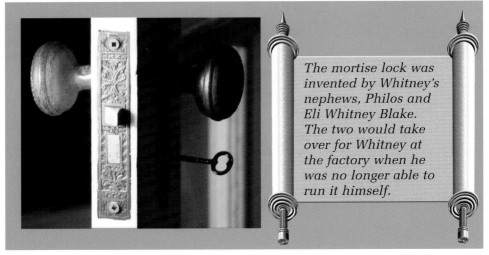

The mortise lock was invented by Whitney's nephews, Philos and Eli Whitney Blake. The two would take over for Whitney at the factory when he was no longer able to run it himself.

lock for his bureau. The lock is described in the memoirs: "The several drawers of his bureaus were locked by a single movement of one key, of a peculiar construction, and an attempt to open any drawer except one would prove ineffectual, even with the right key, which, however, being applied in the proper place, threw all the bolts at one movement."[1]

The Whitneys lived in New Haven with their four children. The youngest, a girl, died at only twenty-one months old. The other girls were Frances and Elizabeth. Their son, Eli Whitney Jr., was born in 1820 and, starting in 1842, would further his father's work on the Whitneyville Armory until the armory closed in 1888.

The former farm boy of Westborough, Massachusetts, had become a successful businessman and a leader in the New Haven community. He promoted banking and development. He encouraged architect Ithiel Town in a new design for a bridge. After receiving a favorable opinion from Whitney, Town patented the wooden truss bridge and built the first one in Connecticut. Along with his friend and former Yale president Ezra Stiles, Whitney was one of the founders of the Connecticut Academy of Arts and Sciences. Chartered in 1799, it is the third oldest of such societies in the United States. Another inventor from Yale was Samuel Morse, who created the telegraph. Morse often worked as a painter. His 1821 portrait of Whitney often accompanies information about Eli Whitney.

His children were still young when Whitney began experiencing pain in September 1822. The pain worsened, and he turned over the running of the armory to his nephews. Philos and Eli Whitney Blake managed the Whitney Armory until 1836.

The doctors told Eli Whitney he had an enlarged prostate. Whitney read up on his disease and consulted with physicians. He analyzed his disease like any other problem he had ever been faced with. He invented a catheter that gave him some relief from pain.

From November 1824, Whitney was in almost constant pain. He died on January 8, 1825, one month after his fifty-ninth birthday. He asked that no fuss be made for his funeral, but people came from all over to New Haven to pay their respects to the great inventor. He was laid to rest at Grove Street Cemetery.

Yale professor and friend Benjamin Silliman said, "With all his contemplative ingenuity and habitual attention to mechanical details, Mr. Whitney did not allow his mind to be narrowed down to a limited horizon. His views of men and things were on the most enlarged scale. The interest of mankind, and especially of his native

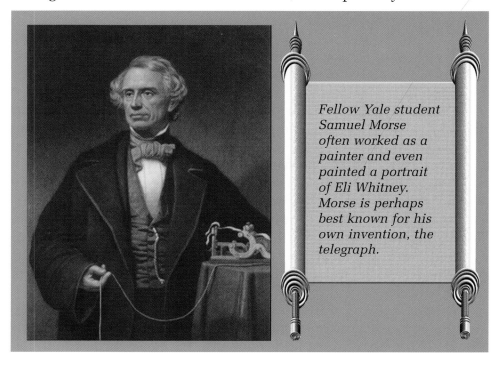

Fellow Yale student Samuel Morse often worked as a painter and even painted a portrait of Eli Whitney. Morse is perhaps best known for his own invention, the telegraph.

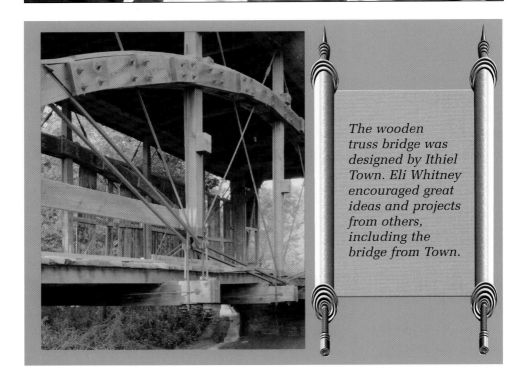

The wooden truss bridge was designed by Ithiel Town. Eli Whitney encouraged great ideas and projects from others, including the bridge from Town.

country, as connected with government, liberty, order, science, arts, literature, morals, and religion, were familiar to his mind, and he delighted in conversing with men of a similar character."[2]

Whitney constantly looked for ways to improve life. Historian Harold Evans called him the godfather of the machine age. Some historians believe that Whitney's innovations to northern industry led to the victory of North over South in the Civil War.

Controversy often surrounds people of greatness, and Whitney was no exception. Other people have been credited with inventing the cotton gin, even Whitney's benefactress, Catharine Greene. Slavery increased in the South after the invention of the cotton gin. By 1810, more than 200,000 people from Africa had been forced into slavery. Other people claimed to use interchangeable parts before he did.

Whitney knew nothing about cotton, and he wasn't a gunsmith. But he did know how to solve problems. His solutions revolutionized industry in the North and the South. His ideas turned complex

Eli Whitney was laid to rest at New Haven's Grove Street Cemetery. He did not want any fuss made at his funeral, but when he died soon after his fifty-ninth birthday, people came from all over the country to pay their respects.

processes into simple steps. The concepts of mass production and assembly lines pushed the United States into the Industrial Revolution, one of the greatest periods of change America has ever experienced. His ideas and his machines were later used to build sewing machines and automobiles. We can still see the benefits of his work today. Eli Whitney was truly a visionary.

The Industrial Revolution

During the nineteenth century, tremedous changes began taking place in the Western world. These changes, both economic and social, came about because of industrialization.

The Industrial Revolution had its earliest beginnings in England during the late 1700s. It spread to other parts of Europe and to North America by the early 1800s. Within a few decades, industrialization was changing work and everyday life for people in Western Europe and the northeastern United States. The United States may have initially lagged behind the British in industrialization, but they would surpass Britain and the rest of the world after the Civil War.

Before the Industrial Revolution, manufacturing was done by hand, animals, or simple machines. People worked in small shops or at home in "cottage industries." The Industrial Revolution took manufacturing out of the home. People moved from rural areas to the cities. Power-driven machines replaced working by hand. Factories became the most economical and efficient way of working.

The introduction of machinery and mass production during the Industrial Revolution created an enormous increase in the production of goods. Eli Whitney wasn't the only one inventing during this time. Others harnessed electricity and invented telephones. Steam power revolutionized transportation, making it easier to travel by boat and train.

Both positive and negative effects came from the Industrial Revolution. The increased production of goods led to increased jobs and a better standard of living for many people. The movement changed the rural, agricultural society of the time into an urban-based industrial society.

Initially, many factories had poor, and sometimes dangerous, working conditions. The amount of hours worked and a person's pay were determined solely by the owners or bosses. Urban areas weren't ready for such large numbers of people. Overcrowding and unsanitary housing were real problems.

Since 1850, unions and labor laws have improved working conditions and wages. This in turn has led to improved housing. Unfortunately, at least one negative result of the Industrial Revolution remains—pollution.

Chapter Notes

Chapter 1   Ten Days That Changed the World

1. While this is a fictionalized conversation, Eli Whitney did meet Phineas Miller and Catherine Greene on the ship to Savannah.

2. Denison Olmsted, *Memoir of Eli Whitney, Esq.* (Reprint of 1832 edition; New York: Arno Publishing Co., 1972), p. 12.

3. Ibid., pp. 13–14.

Chapter 2   Mechanical Genius

1. Denison Olmsted, *Memoir of Eli Whitney, Esq.* (Reprint of 1832 edition; New York: Arno Publishing Co., 1972), p. 6.

2. Dulchie Leimbach "Eli Whitney's Work, and Later Inventions," including interview with Eli Whitney Museum Director William Brown, *New York Times*, January 20, 1995, p. C25.

3. Olmsted, p. 7.

4. Ibid., p. 8.

5. Harold Evans, *They Made America* (Little, Brown and Co., 2004), p. 50.

6. Olmsted, p. 11.

7. The Eli Whitney Museum, "The Factory" http://www.eliwhitney.org/factory.htm

Chapter 3   The Cotton Gin Patent

1. Denison Olmsted, *Memoir of Eli Whitney, Esq.* (Reprint of 1832 edition; New York: Arno Publishing Co., 1972), p. 16.

2. Ibid., pp. 16–17.

3. Ibid., p. 46.

4. National Archives and Records Administration, Records of the United States House of Representatives, Record Group 233: "The Documents." http://www.archives.gov/education/lessons/cotton-gin-patent/#documents

5. U.S. National Archives and Records Administration, Teaching With Documents: "Eli Whitney's Patent for the Cotton Gin" http://www.archives.gov/education/lessons/cotton-gin-patent/

Chapter 4   The Father of Mass Production

1. Benjamin A. Gorman, "Discover Eli Whitney" http://www.yale.edu/ynhti/curriculum/units/1979/3/79.03.03.x.html

2. Denison Olmsted, *Memoir of Eli Whitney, Esq.* (Reprint of 1832 edition; New York: Arno Publishing Co., 1972), p. 48.

3. The Eli Whitney Museum, "The Site" http://www.eliwhitney.org/site.htm

4. The Eli Whitney Museum, "The Arms" http://www.eliwhitney.org/arms.htm

5. The Eli Whitney Museum, "The Factory" http://www.eliwhitney.org/factory.htm

6. The Eli Whitney Museum, "The Arms" http://www.eliwhitney.org/arms.htm

7. Olmsted, p. 48.

Chapter 5   A Visionary

1. Denison Olmsted, *Memoir of Eli Whitney, Esq.* (Reprint of 1832 edition; New York: Arno Publishing Co., 1972), p. 70.

2. Ibid., pp. 73–74.

Chronology

1765   Eli Whitney was born on December 8 in Westborough, Massachusetts

1777   Mother, Elizabeth Whitney, dies in childbirth

1779   Father marries Judith Hazeldon

1781   Starts a business making nails

1789   Enters Yale College

1792   Graduates from Yale

1793   Invents the cotton gin; forms partnership with Phineas Miller; applies for patent

1794   Receives patent 72-X for the cotton gin

1795   Fire destroys cotton gin factory

1796   Delivers 30 cotton gins to Georgia

1797   First patent infringement case heard

1798   Awarded contract to build 10,000 muskets for U.S. government; builds Whitney Armory and introduces method for making interchangeable parts

1801   Sells patent rights to South Carolina

1802   North Carolina and Tennessee taxes use of cotton gin

1803   Phineas Miller dies on December 7

1807   Courts proclaim Eli Whitney as inventor of cotton gin

1812   Applies for patent renewal on cotton gin, but is denied; is awarded second contract with federal government for 15,000 guns

1817   Marries Henrietta Edwards

1820   Eli Whitney Jr. born

1822   Whitney first becomes ill

1825   Dies on January 8

1842   Eli Whitney Jr. furthers his father's work at the Whitney Armory

1888   Whitney Armory is sold to Winchester Arms Company

1832   *Memoir of Eli Whitney, Esq.*, by fellow Yale student Denison Olmsted, is published

Timeline in History

1752	Benjamin Franklin invents lightning rod.
1754	French and Indian War begins in the colonies.
1760	George III becomes King of England.
1762	Six-year-old Wolfgang Amadeus Mozart performs at Vienna's Imperial court.
1765	English chemist Henry Cavendish isolates hydrogen gas.
1769	James Watt patents steam engine.
1774	First Continental Congress meets on September 5 in Philadelphia.
1775	Revolutionary War begins.
1776	Declaration of Independence is signed July 2 and 4.
1787	Constitution of the United States is signed.
1789	George Washington is chosen President of the United States; French Revolution begins.
1790	First patent laws are passed as part of the Constitution.
1792	First *Old Farmer's Almanac* is published.
1793	Thomas Jefferson initiates changes in patent laws that further define what could receive a patent.
1799–1815	Napoleonic wars are fought in Europe.
1796	First presidential election held; John Adams is elected president, Thomas Jefferson is vice president.
1801	Thomas Jefferson begins term as president.
1803	United States acquires Louisiana Purchase on April 30.
1804	Lewis and Clark expedition to explore the West starts May 14.
1808	Beethoven composes famous Fifth Symphony.
1812	War of 1812 is fought between U.S. and Britain; it ends two years later.
1814	George Stephenson designs the first practical steam locomotive.
1830	Andrew Jackson signs the Indian Removal Act; 50,000 Native Americans are forced to migrate to the West from their homes in the South.
1837	Samuel Morse invents the telegraph; the following year he creates Morse code
1845	Elias Howe invents a sewing machine
1861	Abraham Lincoln becomes president; Civil War begins; Louis Pasteur introduces pasteurization.
1863	Battle of Gettysburg is fought.
1865	Civil War ends; President Abraham Lincoln is assassinated.
1867	Alaska is purchased from Russia.
1870	Fifteenth Amendment is passed, giving African Americans the right to vote.
1876	Alexander Graham Bell patents the telephone.

Further Reading

For Young Adults

Mitchell, Barbara. *Maker of Machines: A Story About Eli Whitney* (Creative Minds Biographies). Minneapolis: Carolrhoda Books, 2004.

Patchett, Kaye. *Eli Whitney: Cotton Gin Genius* (Giants of Science). San Diego: Blackbirch Press, 2003.

St. George, Judith. *So You Want to Be An Inventor*. New York: Philomel Books, 2002.

Works Consulted

Dodge, Bertha S. *Cotton—The Plant that Would Be King*. Austin: University of Texas, 1984.

Evans, Harold. *They Made America*. New York, Little Brown & Co., 2004.

Leimbach, Dulchie, "Eli Whitney's Work, and Later Inventions" *New York Times* (January 20, 1995), p. C25.

Olmsted, Denison. *Memoirs of Eli Whitney, Esq.* Reprint of 1832 edition. New York: Arno Press, 1972.

Williams, Trevor. *History of Invention*. Revised edition. New York: Facts on File, 1987.

On the Internet

Eli Whitney Museum, http://www.eliwhitney.org

Lemelson-MIT Program Inventor of the Week: "Eli Whitney; Cotton Gin." http://web.mit.edu/invent/iow/whitney.html

Mulberry Grove Foundation, Inc., Timeline, http://www.mulberrygrove.org/id19.htm

National Archives and Records Administration, Records of the United States, Teaching with Documents: "Eli Whitney's Patent for the Cotton Gin" http://www.archives.gov/education/lessons/cotton-gin-patent/

Smithsonian National Museum of American History Scientists and Inventors: "Model of Eli Whitney's Cotton Gin, About 1800" http://smithsonianlegacies.si.edu/objectdescription.cfm?id=90

United States Patent and Trademark Office, Kids' Pages, Post-Pilgrim Patent Progress USPTO Kids' Pages, "Cotton Gin, March 14, 1794" http://www.uspto.gov/web/offices/ac/ahrpa/opa/kids/themes/pilgrim.htm

United States Patent and Trademark Office, Kids' Pages, "Stories of Creativity," http://www.uspto.gov/web/offices/ac/ahrpa/opa/kids/special/kidstory.html

Glossary

alumnus (uh-LUM-nus)
A person who has been a student at a particular school or college.

artisan (AR-tuh-zun)
Someone who is skilled at working with his or hear hands at a particular craft.

embryonic (em-bree-AH-nik)
Relating to the early stages of growth.

emigrate (EH-muh-grayt)
To leave one's own country in order to live in another country.

gin (JIN)
Short for *engine*; a machine that separates cotton from its seeds.

gristmill (GRIST mil)
A mill for grinding grain.

industrialization (in-DUH-stree-uh-lie-ZAY-shun)
The changing of a society to one that is centered on manufacturing.

infringement (in-FRINJ-mint)
An act contrary to or violating a law or oath; an act done in defiance of another's rights.

memoir (MEM-wahr)
A historical account or biography written from personal knowledge or firsthand sources.

monopoly (muh-NAH-puh-lee)
A group that controls all the sales of a particular product.

patent (PAA-tunt)
A legal document giving the inventor of some item the sole right to manufacture or sell the item.

plantation (plan-TAY-shun)
A large farm for growing crops.

prostate (PRAH-stayt)
A gland surrounding the neck of the bladder in male mammals.

sieve (SIV)
A container with lots of small holes in it, used for separating large pieces from liquid or from small pieces.

textile (TEK-stuhl or TEK-styl)
A fabric or cloth that has been woven or knitted.

visionary (VIH-juh-nay-ree)
Someone who thinks and plans far ahead.

Index